LED BY THE SPIRIT

STUDY GUIDE

Copyright © 2023 by Kent Mattox

Published by Four Rivers Media

All rights reserved. No portion of this book may be reproduced, stored in a retrieval system, or transmitted in any form or by any means—electronic, mechanical, photocopy, recording, scanning, or other—except for brief quotations in critical reviews or articles, without prior written permission of the author.

Scripture quotations are taken from the Holy Bible, New International Version®, NIV®. Copyright © 1973, 1978, 1984, 2011 by Biblica, Inc.™ Used by permission of Zondervan. All rights reserved worldwide. www.zondervan.com. The "NIV" and "New International Version" are trademarks registered in the United States Patent and Trademark Office by Biblica, Inc.™

For foreign and subsidiary rights, contact the author.

Cover design by Simon Parry
Cover photo by Frank Morris, Studio Shot

ISBN: 978-1-959095-86-6   1 2 3 4 5 6 7 8 9 10

Printed in the United States of America

LED BY THE SPIRIT

WHAT **BENNY HINN** TAUGHT ME ABOUT EMPOWERED LIVING

KENT MATTOX

STUDY GUIDE

CONTENTS

Chapter 1. The Spirit Imparts the Supernatural 6

Chapter 2. The Spirit Imparts Boldness............................... 10

Chapter 3. The Spirit Imparts Hunger................................. 14

Chapter 4. The Spirit Imparts the Power of a Personal Relationship... 18

Chapter 5. Activation Through Worship.............................. 22

Chapter 6. Activation Through Submission 26

Chapter 7. Activation Through Generosity........................... 30

Chapter 8. Activation Through Living Out the Word......... 34

Chapter 9. Charting Your Next Chapter 38

LED BY THE SPIRIT

WHAT **BENNY HINN** TAUGHT ME
ABOUT EMPOWERED LIVING

KENT MATTOX

CHAPTER 1

THE SPIRIT IMPARTS THE SUPERNATURAL

"The Lord orchestrates the obedience He requires."

READING TIME

As you read Chapter 1: "The Spirit Imparts the Supernatural" in *Led by the Spirit*, review, reflect on, and respond to the text by answering the following questions.

REVIEW, REFLECT, AND RESPOND

How would you define the supernatural in your own words?

_____
_____
_____
_____
_____

Have you ever doubted what God could do in the midst of your situation? Describe the experience. What made you doubt? How did the circumstance turn out?

_____
_____
_____
_____
_____
_____
_____
_____

What do you think qualifies or disqualifies someone from being used by the Lord? Does God look at us the same way we look at ourselves? Why or why not?

_____
_____
_____
_____
_____

> *"And to know this love that surpasses knowledge—that you may be filled to the measure of all the fullness of God. Now to him who is able to do immeasurably more than all we ask or imagine, according to his power that is at work within us. . . ."*
>
> *Ephesians 3:19-20 (NIV)*

Consider the scripture above and answer the following questions:

What stands out to you from this verse? What do you feel is its meaning?

_____
_____
_____
_____
_____

What does it mean that God's power is "at work within us"?

_____
_____
_____
_____
_____

What stands out to you from the stories told in this chapter?

_____
_____
_____
_____
_____

Do you ever feel like you aren't thinking big enough for the Lord? Explain your answer.

___

How does God prepare us for what He has ahead? Does this road always look the same?

___

What do you feel God is preparing you for in your current season?

___

CHAPTER 2

THE SPIRIT IMPARTS BOLDNESS

"[God] simply needs a willing vessel to step forth, someone who realizes that the spiritual powers are 'on Him' yet the physical presence is all 'on them.'"

READING TIME

As you read Chapter 2: "The Spirit Imparts Boldness" in *Led by the Spirit*, review, reflect on, and respond to the text by answering the following questions.

REVIEW, REFLECT, AND RESPOND

How would you describe boldness in the Holy Spirit? What does this look like? Are you bold in the Spirit?

_____
_____
_____
_____
_____

What do you think bold operation in the Spirit causes? What's stopping you from operating this way?

_____
_____
_____
_____
_____
_____

What does it mean to die to self and live in the Spirit? Are you doing this?

_____
_____
_____
_____
_____
_____

> But the one who prophesies speaks to people for
> their strengthening, encouraging and comfort.
> Anyone who speaks in tongues edifies themselves,
> but the one who prophesies edifies the church.
>
> 1 Corinthians 14:3-4 (NIV)

Consider the scripture above and answer the following questions:

How can your prophesying give strength, encourage, and comfort people?

_____
_____
_____
_____

What do you think is the meaning of this verse? How does speaking in tongues edify the church?

_____
_____
_____
_____
_____
_____

Do you think bold operation in the Spirit is required for the prophesying this verse speaks of? Why or why not?

_____
_____
_____
_____
_____

What are gifts of the Spirit? Do you have any gifts? What are they? Does everyone possess the same gifts of the Spirit?

___

Do you think confidence is important when operating in the Spirit? At what point, if any, does confidence become cockiness?

___

Do you think God purposefully makes situations look like they are not in our favor to show His capability? How do you think He wishes you to react when the odds are seemingly stacked against you?

___

What do you think God needs before one can operate in the Holy Spirit? How should they position their heart?

___

CHAPTER 3

THE SPIRIT IMPARTS HUNGER

"Sometimes, people receive an impartation just by being present where the Holy Spirit is moving."

READING TIME

As you read Chapter 3: "The Spirit Imparts Hunger" in *Led by the Spirit*, review, reflect on, and respond to the text by answering the following questions.

REVIEW, REFLECT, AND RESPOND

What does it mean to impart? Define impartation in your own words.

_____
_____
_____
_____
_____
_____
_____
_____
_____

Of the biblical examples of impartation discussed in this chapter, which is your favorite and why?

_____
_____
_____
_____
_____
_____
_____
_____
_____
_____
_____

> Elisha then picked up Elijah's cloak that had fallen from him and went back and stood on the bank of the Jordan. He took the cloak that had fallen from Elijah and struck the water with it. "Where now is the LORD, the God of Elijah?" he asked. When he struck the water, it divided to the right and to the left, and he crossed over. The company of the prophets from Jericho, who were watching, said, "The spirit of Elijah is resting on Elisha." And they went to meet him and bowed to the ground before him.
>
> *2 Kings 2:13–15 (NIV)*

Consider the scripture above and answer the following questions:

What is powerful about the above verse, which takes place after Elijah's ascent?

_____
_____
_____
_____
_____

Why did the prophets from Jericho bow down to Elisha?

_____
_____
_____
_____

Why is relationship an essential ingredient of most impartation?

_____
_____
_____
_____

What is another way, besides relationship, that impartation occurs?

Have you ever let your fear of the enemy guide you? What was the result?

Can impartation be evil as well? Why or why not?

What do you think needs to happen in the heart of the "impartee" before impartation occurs?

CHAPTER 4

THE SPIRIT IMPARTS THE POWER OF A PERSONAL RELATIONSHIP

"The Spirit not only is everywhere, the Spirit also knows all things."

READING TIME

As you read Chapter 4: "The Spirit Imparts the Power of a Personal Relationship" in *Led by the Spirit*, rreview, reflect on, and respond to the text by answering the following questions.

REVIEW, REFLECT, AND RESPOND

What does it mean to have intimacy with the Holy Spirit? Is this a one-time decision or an ongoing mindset?

_____
_____
_____
_____

What is the "quickening of the Spirit"? Have you ever experienced this before? If so, what was it like?

_____
_____
_____
_____
_____

Do you have a personal relationship with the Holy Spirit? Do you seek to simply understand the Holy Spirit, or to know Him personally?

_____
_____
_____
_____
_____

> *Where can I go from your Spirit? Where can I flee from your presence? If I go up to the heavens, you are there; if I make my bed in the depths, you are there. If I rise on the wings of dawn, if I settle on the far side of the sea, even there your hand will guide me, your right hand will hold me fast.*
>
> *Psalm 139:7–10 (NIV)*

Consider the scripture above and answer the following questions:

What does this verse reveal about God's presence?

_____
_____
_____
_____
_____

Does God distance Himself from us when we sin? Why or why not?

_____
_____
_____
_____

What in your life do you need to change in order to operate as if God is always with you?

_____
_____
_____
_____
_____

What is the extent of the Holy Spirit's knowledge? Knowing this, do you ever think there is a time or situation where you cannot or should not trust the Holy Spirit's guidance?

_____
_____
_____
_____

How do you think the Holy Spirit has changed over the years? Why do you think this is the case?

_____
_____
_____
_____

What does the Holy Spirit sound like? How do you know you are hearing Him and not the voice of the enemy?

_____
_____
_____
_____

What practical steps can you take today to draw nearer in your relationship to the Holy Spirit?

_____
_____
_____
_____

CHAPTER 5

ACTIVATION THROUGH WORSHIP

"In the same way negative music shifts our spirits in certain ways, the soundtrack of praise elevates us to live at a higher level."

READING TIME

As you read Chapter 5: "Activation Through Worship" in Led by the Spirit, review, reflect on, and respond to the text by answering the following questions.

REVIEW, REFLECT, AND RESPOND

What is worship? Define worship in your own words.

_____
_____
_____
_____
_____
_____

Why do you worship? Is worship external, internal, or a mix of both?

_____
_____
_____
_____
_____
_____
_____
_____

How powerful is worship? Do you think worship can change our lives? Why or why not?

_____
_____
_____
_____
_____
_____
_____

> *Praise the LORD, my soul; all my inmost being, praise his holy name. Praise the LORD, my soul, and forget not all his benefits—who forgives all your sins and heals all your diseases, who redeems your life from the pit and crowns you with love and compassion. . . .*
>
> *Psalm 103:1–5 (NIV)*

Consider the scripture above and answer the following questions:

Why do you think David is passionately praising the Lord in this Psalm?

_____
_____
_____
_____
_____

What do you think David means when he writes about God, "who redeems your life from the pit"?

_____
_____
_____
_____
_____

When and where does worship take place? Is worship something that only takes place in the church on Sunday mornings?

_____
_____

What does it mean to create an "atmosphere of worship"? How can you create a worship atmosphere in your work, home, and day-to-day life?

Do you see worship as a duty or as a privilege? Explain your answer.

How can you worship God through what you say and how you act?

CHAPTER 6

ACTIVATION THROUGH SUBMISSION

"When you walk in submission, you're actually more free to learn."

READING TIME

As you read Chapter 6: "Activation Through Submission" in *Led by the Spirit*, rreview, reflect on, and respond to the text by answering the following questions.

REVIEW, REFLECT, AND RESPOND

What does it mean to submit to God? Have you fully submitted to God in every area of your life?

_____
_____
_____
_____
_____
_____

Do you submit to any authority besides God? If so, who? Why do you do this?

_____
_____
_____
_____
_____

Why is it important to submit? What happens when we have hard hearts and are unwilling to submit to God and the authority He places in our lives?

_____
_____
_____
_____
_____
_____
_____

> The centurion replied, "Lord, I do not deserve to have you come under my roof. But just say the word, and my servant will be healed. For I myself am a man under authority, with soldiers under me." When Jesus heard this, he was amazed and said to those following him, "Truly I tell you, I have not found anyone in Israel with such great faith."
>
> *Matthew 8:8–10 (NIV)*

Consider the scripture above and answer the following questions:

What about what the centurion said to Jesus made Jesus marvel at his faith?

_____
_____
_____
_____

What do you think is the purpose of this verse? What can you learn from it?

_____
_____
_____
_____
_____

What is spiritual submission? What does this look like in practice?

_____
_____
_____
_____
_____

What does it truly mean to honor your father and mother? Do you do this currently? How can you show them greater honor?

_____
_____
_____
_____

How does submitting to someone else allow us to learn more? Explain.

_____
_____
_____
_____

Who in your life are you currently submitted to, besides God? What made you choose them?

_____
_____
_____
_____

CHAPTER 7

ACTIVATION THROUGH GENEROSITY

"If boldness is the key to unlocking God's power, then generosity is the key to unlocking everything else."

READING TIME

As you read Chapter 7: "Activation Through Generosity" in *Led by the Spirit*, review, reflect on, and respond to the text by answering the following questions.

REVIEW, REFLECT, AND RESPOND

How do you define generosity in your own words? Does being generous only mean generosity with finances?

___

Who benefits the most from generosity? The giver, the receiver, or both parties? Explain your answer.

___

Do you or have you ever had an issue with money? What does an issue with money entail? How can you defend against this moving forward?

___

> *No one can serve two masters. Either you will hate the one and love the other, or you will be devoted to the one and despise the other. You cannot serve both God and money.*
>
> *Matthew 6:24 (NIV)*

Consider the scripture above and answer the following questions:

Why do you think it is impossible to serve two masters at the same time?

_____
_____
_____
_____

How can you be sure your love for God is always greater than your love and desire for money?

_____
_____
_____
_____

What does it look like when someone lives with money as their master?

_____
_____
_____
_____

What do you think our generosity demonstrates to those around us?

_____
_____
_____
_____

Do you think you can determine the state of someone's heart based upon their generosity (or lack thereof)? Why or why not?

_____
_____
_____
_____
_____

What do you think generosity "unlocks" when practiced correctly? Is this true for your life?

_____
_____
_____
_____

CHAPTER 8

ACTIVATION THROUGH LIVING OUT THE WORD

"'If your Bible is falling apart, you're not,' Doc often said."

READING TIME

As you read Chapter 8: "Activation Through Living Out the Word" in *Led by the Spirit*, review, reflect on, and respond to the text by answering the following questions.

REVIEW, REFLECT, AND RESPOND

Do you do your best to live out God's Word? In what area could you better live out His Word?

_____
_____
_____
_____
_____
_____

What do you think we gain from living out God's Living Word? How do we personally benefit?

_____
_____
_____
_____
_____
_____

What is your daily routine for getting into God's Word? How could you improve?

_____
_____
_____
_____
_____
_____

> *I have hidden your word in my heart that
> I might not sin against you.*
>
> *Psalm 119:11 (NIV)*

Consider the scripture above and answer the following questions:

What do you think it means to "hide" God's Word in one's heart?

_____
_____
_____
_____
_____
_____

What do you think David meant when he wrote this Psalm? Is this applicable to your own life?

_____
_____
_____
_____
_____
_____

How can hiding God's Word in our heart stop us from sinning?

_____
_____
_____
_____
_____

Do you think our daily habits of getting in the Word of God and how we live are directly correlated? Why or why not?

How does one receive revelation from God's Word? Is there a process?

What happens when one prioritizes reading, studying, and meditating upon the Word of God?

How can you make more space and time for God's Word in your life? What do you need to set aside?

CHAPTER 9

CHARTING YOUR NEXT CHAPTER

"It hit me: if my Lord Jesus willingly took the form of servanthood, I certainly could as well."

READING TIME

As you read Chapter 9: "Charting Your Next Chapter" in *Led by the Spirit*, review, reflect on, and respond to the text by answering the following questions.

REVIEW, REFLECT, AND RESPOND

If you had to guess, what does the next chapter of your life hold? Are you open to God guiding you elsewhere?

_____
_____
_____
_____
_____
_____
_____
_____
_____
_____

Have you ever felt like God's timing was late or ill-timed? Do you ever have trouble trusting God's timing over your own?

_____
_____
_____
_____
_____
_____
_____
_____
_____
_____

> *Therefore if you have any encouragement from being united with Christ, if any comfort from his love, if any common sharing in the Spirit, if any tenderness and compassion, then make my joy complete by being like-minded, having the same love, being one in spirit and of one mind.*
>
> *Philippians 2:1-2 (NIV)*

Consider the scripture above and answer the following questions:

What do you feel is the meaning of this verse?

_____
_____
_____
_____
_____

How can you apply this verse to your life?

_____
_____
_____
_____
_____

What does it mean to "be one in spirit and of one mind"? Do you feel the church currently meets this standard?

_____
_____
_____
_____
_____

How do you know when it is time to reap? How do you shift your stance in times of reaping versus times of sowing?

_____
_____
_____
_____

Which of the seven revelations listed at the end of this chapter stick out to you and why? Which do you need to work on better embodying through your life and actions?

_____
_____
_____
_____

What is your biggest takeaway from Led by the Spirit? How can you use this takeaway to develop a practical action plan?

_____
_____
_____
_____

www.ingramcontent.com/pod-product-compliance
Lightning Source LLC
Chambersburg PA
CBHW070654100426
42734CB00048B/2989